THE ANIMALS OF

DREAMWORKS

KUNG FU PANDA

Popcorn
ELT
Readers

New Words

beautiful

The girl is **beautiful**.

fight

The girls are **fighting**.

brave

She's very **brave**!

jump

It can **jump**.

look after

He **looks after** his dog.

strong

The man is **strong**.

mountains

These **mountains** are very big.

tail

The cat has a long **tail**.

Where's the popcorn?
Look in your book.
Can you find it?

THE ANIMALS OF DreamWorks KUNG FU PANDA

Po is a **panda**. He loves kung fu. He is always hungry!

Giant pandas live in the **mountains** of China. They eat **bamboo**.

bamboo

Tigress is a tiger. She is very **brave**. She is a good friend.

Tigers are **beautiful**. There are not many tigers in China now.

Crane does not like to **fight**. But he is very good at kung fu.

leg

Cranes have very long **legs**. They can walk in the water.

Monkey is funny and he is good at kung fu.

Monkeys have long **tails**. They **jump** from **tree** to **tree**.

tree

Mantis is small, but he is very quick.

Viper always **looks after** her friends. She is **strong**.

Can you see a viper and a mantis?

They are green and live in **trees**.

Master Shifu is a red panda. He is a kung fu teacher.

Red pandas are quiet animals. They come out at night.

Tai Lung is a snow leopard. He is **strong** and he is bad.

Snow leopards live in the **mountains**. They have long **tails** and they like to **jump**.

All of these animals live in China.

China

All of these animals love kung fu!

THE END

After you read

1 Colour the words.

animals = verbs =

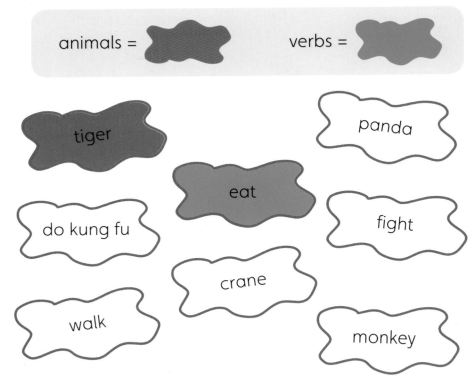

tiger

panda

eat

do kung fu

fight

crane

walk

monkey

2 Work with a friend. Choose an animal and a verb from exercise 1. Can your friend do the mime?

Can you walk like a panda?

Yes, I can!

3 Which animal is it?

mantis   monkey   ~~red panda~~   tiger   viper

a

red panda
·······························

b
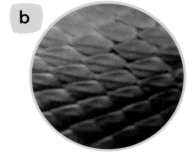

c

·······························

·······························

d

e
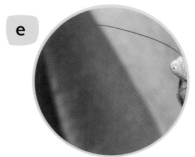

·······························

·······························

4 Match the sentences with the pictures.

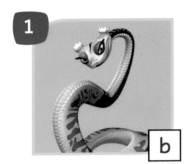 **1** **b**

 **2**

a) He has long legs.

b) She looks after her friends.

c) He is a good teacher.

d) He is always hungry!

e) He is bad.

 **3**

 **5**

 **4**

Quiz time!

Read the sentences. Answer Yes or No.

		Yes	No
1	Snow leopards live in the mountains.	✓	☐
2	Red pandas come out at night.	☐	☐
3	There are many tigers in China now.	☐	☐
4	Vipers live in trees.	☐	☐
5	Giant pandas are green.	☐	☐

SCORES

How many of your answers are correct?

0–2: Read the book again! Can you answer the questions now?

3–4: Good work! You like Po and his friends!

5: Wow! You love animals!

Chant

1 🎵 **Listen and read.**

All of these animals

All of these animals
Love kung fu!
Funny or strong,
Small or long,
All of these animals
Love kung fu!

2 🎵 **Say the chant.**